Contents

Introduction 3
Road racing 5
Starting out 7
  Joining a club 7
  Entering a road race 8
  Licences 8
  Competition categories 9
  Choosing your race 9
Equipment 10
  Clothing 12
Preparation 13
Criteriums 14
Closed circuits 15
Single-day racing 16
Stage racing 18
  Variations on a theme 18
Time trialling 20
Track racing 22

Equipment 24
  Clothing 25
Sprinting 26
Handicap racing 29
Kilo 29
Tandem sprinting 30
Pursuiting 31
Distance events 33
Madison 36
Six-day racing 37
Motor-pace 38
Keirin 40
Riding in a bunch 41
Training 42
Drugs 43
Glossary – bike talk 44
Useful addresses 46
Index 48

Time-trialling action from Italy's Gianni Bugno ▶

Conversion table

	multiply by:
yards → metres	0.9144
metres → yards	1.0936
miles → kilometres	1.6093
kilometres → miles	0.6214

Acknowledgements

Text by Roger St Pierre.
The publishers would like to thank Jim Hendry of the British Cycling Federation and Jo Tym of the English Schools Cycling Association.

Photographs on the outside covers, the inside covers, and on pages 1, 2, 4, 6, 7, 9, 11, 12, 13, 19, 21, 22, 23, 31, 32, 37, 42 and 47 courtesy of Allsport UK Ltd; on pages 5, 17, 41, 43 and 46 courtesy of Sporting Pictures (UK) Ltd; on pages 12, 14, 33, 34, 38 and 40 courtesy of Phil O'Connor; on pages 15 and 25 courtesy of Gerard Brown; on pages 20, 24, 26, 27, 28, 29, 30, 35, 36, 39 and 45 courtesy of the author.
Illustration on page 10 by Walter Molino.

Note Throughout the book cyclists are referred to individually as 'he'. This should be taken to mean 'he or she' where appropriate. Note also that French is the international language of cycle racing. A glossary can be found on page 44.

Introduction

If horse racing is the sport of kings, then surely cycling is the king of sports. Anon

Cycling is the world's second most popular sport after soccer. The annual drama of the Tour de France entertains television audiences around the globe, while an estimated 17 million fans flock to watch the great three-week race from the roadside.

The single-day classics, such as Paris–Roubaix, the Tour of Lombardy and the annual world championships exert similar pulling power. Across Europe, villages and towns celebrate their annual cycling events; the highlights of their local year.

The pace doesn't let up in winter, when the indoor board tracks rattle to the spinning wheels of the great six-day races, and hordes of warmly-clad spectators plod out into the fields and woods to watch cyclo-cross riders battle through mud and slush.

In Japan, the thrilling brand of cycle track racing known as *keirin* produces more gambling revenue in a single day than is generated in a whole season of British and French horse racing. The proceeds are channelled into schools, health facilities and other public projects.

In the USA too, cycling's popularity continues to grow, thanks to the international success of the nation's top riders, while South Americans are positively fanatical in their enthusiasm for the sport.

Indeed, such is cycling's international appeal, that it has been a core sport in the Olympics ever since Baron De Coubertin started the modern movement at the turn of the century.

But fun though it is to watch, cycling is, more importantly, a wonderful activity actually to participate in. Besides being a great way of getting about, keeping fit and healthy at the same time, cycling is truly a sport for all. It comprises many different disciplines to suit all shapes, sizes, characters and individual strengths. Thus the heavily-muscled sprinter, who can scorch ahead over the final 200 m of a track race, would trail minutes behind over the big mountains; conversely, the wiry little climber, who dances so easily up the steepest Alpine slopes, would be lapped many times in a track madison race.

Moreover, there are few sports in which such disparate age groups are catered for. Juvenile racing attracts riders as young as five, while 80-year-olds can still figure among the prize winners in veteran events with age-related handicap systems.

Girls and women compete alongside boys and men, as well as in specialised races. The disabled too can take part, with blind riders serving as 'stokers' on tandems, and even one-armed and one-legged cyclists racing against more able-bodied participants.

Cycle racing is a unique combination of the mechanical, physical and mental (tactics are crucial for victory). It offers thrills and spills, while demanding dedication, training, courage and determination. But everyone can take part at their own level, the sport being geared to cater for different abilities and degrees of dedication.

At top level, cycling is becoming increasingly a worldwide sport. However, its image is still something of a Cinderella. Although cycling is consistently among the top five competitor sports, it has tended to attract little attention from the media, general public and schools. Factors are now combining to change this. Technological advancement in cycle manufacturing, the continued development of bicycle trails nationwide, and the growth in popularity of mountain biking are all helping to raise cycle racing's profile.

Competitive cycling is multi–dimensional, including such disparate disciplines as road and track racing, time trialling, mountain biking, downhilling, cyclo–cross, BMX, cycle speedway, and even ball games like cycle ball and bicycle polo. Bringing all these

activities together simply because they all use bicycles makes no more sense than trying to treat all ball games as a single sport. While some cyclists will try everything, most 'bikies' specialise in just one or two aspects of the game. Consequently this book is geared to dealing specifically with road racing and track sport. Although time trialling is actually the backbone of American cycle sport, meriting a book of its own, there is only space here for a brief exposition.

Road racing

Modern cycle road racing began in the late Victorian era. The first recorded competition was held in the Parc St Cloud, Paris, on 31 May 1868, and covered just 1200 m, from the fountains to the park gates and back. It was won by the English-born vet, James Moore, who in November 1870 also won the oldest of amateur classics, the Paris–Rouen.

The epic Bordeaux–Paris marathon was founded in 1891 and was soon followed by Liege–Bastogne–Liege, Milan–San Remo, Paris–Roubaix, the Tour of Flanders, The Tour of Lombardy and most of the other one-day professional classics.

It was in 1903 that newspaper editor Henri Desgranges created the Tour de France in a bid to increase circulation. The 78 competitors faced a 1510 mile route, split into six stages separated by a number of rest days. It started on 1 July and finished on the 19th, taking in such towns as Lyons, Marseille, Toulouse, Bordeaux and Nantes, before finishing back in Paris.

The famed yellow jersey of the race leader was introduced in 1921 and has become one of the best known symbols in all sport. Its colour reflects that of the paper used by Desgranges' *L'Auto* publication.

Today the Tour ranks with soccer's World Cup as the greatest of all single sport events in terms of both live and TV spectators. Its stage-racing format has been copied for a range of other cycle racing events.

Road racing provides an infinite variety of competition. Courses range from tight criteriums round narrow village streets, to wide-open airfield circuits. Some races are flat, others scale the highest mountain passes. The bone-jarring cobbles of Paris–Roubaix contrast with the smooth tarmac of the purpose-built Eastway circuit in East London. Some one-day races are over in minutes, while others last for hours. Distances can range from the 10 km of

▲ *Spain's Pedro Delgado in the famed yellow jersey of the Tour de France*

◄ *The notorious 'Hell of the North' cobbles of the Paris–Roubaix*

many juvenile events to the 572 km of Bordeaux–Paris, which used to start at midnight and finish in the late afternoon. The weather too can vary dramatically from gale-force winds and torrential rain to freezing cold or scorching heat.

Single-day cycle road racing is a classic athletic sport, being run on a massed-start, first-across-the-line-wins format.

The stage racing of the big tours, with its chessboard tactics, adds another dimension. The winner is the rider with the lowest aggregate time over the various stages, rather than the first rider to the finish on the last stage. The race leader at the start of each stage is usually awarded a special, distinctive jersey to wear (commonly referred to as the yellow jersey, though it may be another colour). Time bonuses add further complication, with riders finishing in the first three places on a stage having bonus time allowances deducted from their overall times. There is often also a separate points classification, decided on aggregate placings rather than time. What's more, most stage races will include at least one time trial (individual riders against the clock) as well as massed-start stages.

Group training builds fitness and team cameraderie ▶

Starting out

Cycle road racing is a very demanding sport, so you will need to reach a fairly high level of fitness before entering your first race. Besides training on your bike, swimming, rowing, skiing, gym work and similar physical activities can be a great help. Do be careful though of excessive running, as the leg muscles are used in a different way, and the jarring effect of hard surfaces can cause problems.

Joining a club

While many riders train alone, going out in a group on club runs or with 'chain gangs' (informal training groups) will hone your speed, get you used to following a wheel, and teach you to ride safely and efficiently in a group. You will also learn all about 'bit and bit', where riders take turns at making the pace.

In addition to joining national organisations such as the U.S. Cycling Federation (USCF) as a private member, you may join a local cycling club. Ask your nearest specialist bike shop or people at a local race meeting about clubs in your area. The USCF can also refer you to the district representative in your area to obtain information on local events.

Some clubs exist purely as racing teams. Novices are better advised to join an organisation that also offers regular social gatherings, club runs and other activities, and where there are older members to pass on advice. For lesser riders, belonging to a sponsored club usually offers little benefit other than reflected glory and occasional discounts on race clothing.

Entering a road race

Before riding your first road race, enter a few time trials in order to gain some measure of your abilities. No licence is required for most amateur road races, but you will most likely need to be registered in advance.

For a list of road races, rules and regulations, consult your USCF district representative or visit a nearby specialist bike shop.

Licences

Depending on the race you wish to enter, licencing requirements will vary. Most amateur races in the U.S. do not require licencing. However, as your skills progress, you may decide to pursue professional or specialised racing (such as mountain biking), which may carry different requirements. Beginners and occasional racers can obtain one–day licences if required, but most events today take entries 'on the line.'

In advance, USCF entry fees are about $10 per race for amateurs, depending primarily on prize lists and race location. Prices may increase if entries are bought on the line, but they should not exceed $15. These charges help pay for the organisation, changing facilities, and prizes, and also include the cost of personal and group insurance. If a race is sponsored by a private organisation, entry fees will vary because they are not regulated by the USCF.

Competition categories

Under USCF rules, competitors are banded into divisions and categories. These start with the Midget Division (ages 9–12) and progress through the Intermediate Division (12–18), the Junior Division (14–18), and four categories of the Senior Division. Each member must have reached the lowest age and not yet the highest age in their division or category by January 1 of the current year. The category jumps in the Senior Division are earned through membership in the USCF of at least a year and through a points score system dependent on finishing in the first six in races. It is possible to jump straight from junior to second category. Cycling is currently moving toward 'single class' status, abolishing the distinctions between amateurs and the pro ranks, so that both compete together on equal terms. There is also a Veteran Division for any rider over the age of 40, although they may continue to compete in first, second or third categories (or indeed professional races), depending on their level of ability.

Junior, Intermediate, and Midget riders may be divided into separate groups for boys and girls. They are also subject to gear restrictions. The USCF Annual Rule Book lists the gear limits for each division.

Cycling is truly a sport for all – the Tour Feminin arouses the same enthusiasm as its male version ▶

Choosing your race

When choosing your first races, don't be over-ambitious. It is better to enter a relatively short event on an easy 'fish and chipper' course, than to dive in at the deep end with a hilly event likely to attract the 'big hitter' riders. After all, it is not much fun trailing minutes behind the bunch. Take the opportunity to learn the ropes and get a true measure of your abilities, rather than tearing along only to tire long before the race is over.

Equipment

An increasingly competitive, commercial environment plus high-tech advances have led to enormous progress in racing cycle design over recent years.

Today's cycle racing stars insist on the best and latest in technology, forever trying out new refinements. We have seen brake levers with hidden cables and incorporated gear controls, disc wheels, tri-spokes and aerospokes, straight front forks, eight-speed freewheel blocks, monocoque track frames, and so on.

Yet it remains fact that a bike is a bike, and a good rider mounted on an old-fashioned model could still be competitive on most courses. Those of modest means need not therefore be put off competing. While no-one today

The legendary Fausto Coppi ▶

is likely to win their first novice race on a butcher's bike, as the great Italian rider Fausto Coppi did. Cheaper models can hold their own alongside expensive superbikes in most road race bunches. Cycling can prove one of the more expensive sports, but it is possible to do it on a tight budget too.

Beware, however, that many cheap bikes sold as 'racers' by chain stores are fakes. It pays to go to specialist shops for proper advice not only on the type of bike, but also on the correct size and riding position.

The choice of 12, 14 or 16 gears is a matter of budget, but it is advisable to trade up where possible, as the more expensive group sets offer smoother, more reliable transmission. A good saddle and the best affordable wheels can also make a real difference.

Keep your bike clean and your chain and bearings properly lubricated. Tyre pressures are important, with 9 bar (or around 125 lbs psi) suitable for most conditions. On wet roads, let a little air out.

France's Laurent Jalabert replaces lost energy on the move ▶

Never ride with bent pedals, as they can cause serious knee problems. Today clipless pedals have taken over from the toeclips and straps of the past (except among some track sprinters). Check shoe cleats for proper alignment and replace them if worn, as numerous races have been lost through riders pulling their feet off the pedals when sprinting for the line.

Race food, such as fruit, fig rolls, or crustless brown-bread sandwiches of ham or jam, should be carried in jersey pockets. Nowadays, though, most riders take their food in the liquid form of energy drinks. Feeding bottles are held by special bottle cages attached to down or seat tubes.

Clothing

Points of contact (hands, feet and backside) are of crucial importance. Saddle soreness is an occupational hazard, which can be avoided by a combination of good hygiene, the right saddle, and racing shorts fitted with a top-quality chamois or synthetic insert. Track mitts with a leather palm not only prevent blisters, but also protect against grazed hands in the event of a fall. Shoes should be comfortable and well kept. Buy the best pair that you can afford, and wear them with clean, smart ankle socks.

Today's road racing jerseys are made of material that 'breathes', such as lycra, with pockets at the rear for carrying food, sponges and extra drinks in longer races.

In cold weather wear armwarmers, a long-sleeve jersey, legwarmers or tights, thermal or ski gloves, and overshoes; cold muscles do not function properly and can easily be strained. A newspaper or plastic bag stuffed up the front of the jersey will keep chill winds out and can be readily discarded. A racing cape is another useful piece of kit in heavy rain.

Hardshell crash helmets are now compulsory in all American road and track races. It is important to buy the correct size, though special foam pads can be added to make fine adjustments. Leather 'hairnet' style crash helmets are no longer permissible.

Many riders use trendy sunglasses, even when it's dull. These do serve a purpose other than looking good. Besides eliminating glare, they help keep dirt, grit and insects out of the eyes while racing.

Preparation

Cyclists *do* shave their legs for several reasons: legs covered with massage oil attract dust and dirt, so unshaven limbs are more likely to pick up infection; and should you be unlucky enough to crash, plasters are even more painful to remove from hairy legs. But perhaps most importantly of all, they look scruffy, and 'bikies' do tend to be incorrigible poseurs!

Pre-race massage is good, as long as it is carried out by a trained professional. Failing that, some massage oil gently rubbed into legs and arms will help ward off cramp and improve the tan! In early season events, when the cold and wet can be a real problem, a coating of embrocation or olive oil mixed with a proprietary heating agent such as Deep Heat or Born can be invaluable. However, take care to wash any residue from your hands before going to the toilet!

Legs shaven, oiled and ready for action! ▶

Make sure your bike is clean and functioning properly. You will need to get it checked by the official machine examiner before being allowed to sign on and collect your race number. It is, however, still your own responsibility to make sure the gears work properly, that tyres are stuck on well, and that your back wheel will not pull over under effort.

On arrival at race headquarters, memorise the route, the number of laps, location of finish and other pertinent details. If possible, reconnoitre the course in advance.

Allow yourself a good hour for the rituals of machine examination (juveniles and juniors will be subject to a gear check), signing on, changing into race clothing, and a brisk five to ten-minute warm-up (but don't stray too far from the start). Also visit the toilet, as there's nothing worse than being caught short during a race.

On the line, try to get into one of the front rows, especially if the race is on a small circuit. It's worth sprinting away for the first few yards to get clear of the mêlée, avoiding crashes at the start or someone's pedal in your spokes. It's a shame to be out of a race when it has hardly begun.

Criteriums

Races on small, tight circuits closed to other traffic are generally known as criteriums, or 'crits' for short. In the U.S. these may be anything between 500m and 3 or 4km, though in Europe the circuits are likely to be a bit longer.

The primary focus of criteriums is on time—running a short, fast race—as opposed to distance racing.

Crits are high speed affairs, where the ability to corner fast is vital. Though strong men sometimes break clear and lap the field, usually such races are down to a hectic, no–holds–barred, sprint finish. Aces will make sure they are placed in the first three or four going into the last lap, and will aim to go into the final corner either in the lead or in second place, relying on their powerful jump out of the corner to carry them to victory.

In such action-packed races it is vital to stay near the front of the pack at all times. Those at the back have a far harder time as the bunch stretches like a rubber band after each corner.

◀ *The high speed action of criterium racing makes it a great spectator sport*

Closed circuits

Closed circuits are probably the best starting point for the newcomer to racing. Events are held on airfields, industrial estates, motor-racing circuits (such as Brands Hatch, Goodwood and Castle Combe), around public parks and on purpose-built courses (such as Eastway in East London, and Birmingham Wheels). Each provides a different challenge. Park circuits, for example, are often narrow and twisty, with hazards such as errant pedestrians and dogs. In contrast, airfields are usually flat, wide and safe, though sometimes windswept.

With no traffic to worry about, riders can use the whole width of the circuit, allowing bigger fields than could be accommodated on open roads. (The famous early-season Aintree Gallop attracts well over 200 entries each year.)

In road and circuit events a yellow flag is used to mark the final 200 m, and a chequered flag is waved at the finish line. 'Primes', special mid-race sprints often at the top of a climb or on a pre-determined lap, are denoted by a white flag. A bell usually indicates the start of the last lap, and a hooter warns of a next-lap prime. On circuits a lap board can be displayed prominently in the finishing straight.

The traffic-free, wide open spaces of London's purpose-built Eastway circuit enable safe cycling

Single-day racing

Most bike racing is held on the open road over a single stage, with every event and course having a character of its own. Some will suit sprinters, some climbers, some end in a massed-bunch sprint, others with riders straggled all over the countryside.

Under the terms of the Road Traffic Acts, all cycle road races require prior police approval. Official vehicles are on hand to warn approaching road traffic, and sometimes there is also a police escort. For major events a rolling road-closure (as is normal on the Continent) may be imposed, with police stopping oncoming traffic at the roadside and waving following traffic past when it is safe. Nevertheless, riders must still observe the rules of the road, although conditions nowadays are considerably more relaxed than in former, less sport-friendly times, when riders were actually prosecuted for crossing white lines, failing to put their feet down at stop signs and exceeding speed limits.

Juvenile races are not allowed on the open road, and junior events are restricted to a distance of 100 km. Exceptions are the National Championship and the National Junior Road Race Series events, which may cover up to 120 km.

Where 100 to 120 mile road races were once common in the UK and Ireland, nowadays these tend to be between 65 and 80 miles. On the Continent, on the other hand, the major professional classics and the world professional road title are run over courses of between 140 and 180 miles. Such long races have one or more feeding zones en route, where team helpers are allowed to hand up *musettes* (cotton bags containing foods) and *bidons* (feeding bottles).

Road racing is a highly tactical sport, in which team-mates or even rivals will often ride in common cause. Sprinters will try to sit in and do as little work as possible, saving themselves for the finish; strong men will aim to break away, either alone or in a small group; and climbers will hope to excel whenever the gradient steepens. Good places to attack are just as the bunch relaxes after a former break is brought back, coming out of a corner, or as riders ease over the top of a climb.

The thrilling spectacle of a road race ▶

Stage racing

This is cycle sport at its most glamorous, with the great national tours being among the most gruelling sporting events in the world. Today's Tour de France, for example, covers more than 2,000 miles over a three-week period, with average speeds of close to 25 mph.

A strong back-up team helps in any road race. In stage races it is essential, explaining why the Tour de France winner traditionally distributes his entire winnings to his team-mates. (He then makes his money from dramatic increases in start fees in minor races, sponsorship and product endorsement contracts.)

Besides the tours there are countless smaller stage races. These range in length from a couple of stages within a single day to a race of seven to ten days duration. Most though are held over three or four days. Apart from the many professional events, stage races are also organised for amateurs, women, and even juveniles (on closed roads), juniors and veterans.

Each stage is run as a self-contained race, usually with its own prizes. To decide the race leader (and eventually the overall winner), the times for all the preceding stages are added together. Sometimes time bonuses are awarded for stage placings or mid-stage sprints. These are deducted from the riders' aggregate times when calculating the classification tables.

A separate points classification also often exists. Each rider's finishing positions on the individual stages are added together, the points winner being the rider with the lowest total.

In many events there is a 'King of the Mountains' (or 'King of the Hills') classification, points being awarded for the first riders to the top of various climbs in the race.

Variations on a theme

Occasionally road races are run on a handicap basis. Instead of all starting together, riders are sent off in groups according to their category (juniors first, then second and third category riders, and finally first cats and pros). As most races in Australia are run in such fashion, such events are commonly called Australian pursuits.

In France and Spain, uphill races are sometimes held. Often in two stages, the first finds riders tackling the stage on their own in time-trial fashion, with the second being held as a massed-start, bunch race.

Tour de France drama from Robert Millar and Pedro Delgado ▶

Time trialling

Time trialling merits a book of its own, being a separate and specialist discipline. However, since it plays a part in most stage-race formats, a brief explanation is included here.

Devised in Victorian Britain, time-trialling events at that time were cloaked in secrecy to avoid confrontation with the authorities, who were vigorously opposed to cycle racing on the roads. Riders would be prosecuted for 'riding furiously so as to endanger the life and limb of passengers on the Queen's highway'.

The time-trial format consists of riders competing 'alone and unpaced', being sent off by the starter at regular intervals (a minute under British Road Time Trials Council rules) and timed individually over the distance. Riders who are caught have to give way to their overtakers and are penalised if they take pace.

Sometimes called 'The Race of Truth', a time trial certainly does sort the men from the boys. But it can also be inherently unfair, as riders in a large field can start as much as two hours apart, sometimes facing totally different weather and traffic conditions.

Time trialling has long been the cornerstone of British competitive cycling, as shown in this shot from the 1930s

▲ *Well drilled formations in a team time trial*

When seconds count, concentration is everything for the time trialist ▶

A refinement is the team time trial, in which teams rather than individuals are sent off at intervals, the finishing time usually being that of the third team member to cross the line. The essence of such events is joint and cohesive effort. Ace teams ride in close formation to optimise wind shelter, with each rider going through smoothly for his turn at the front, before swinging off and dropping back to rejoin the rear of the group.

Track racing

Cycle tracks (or velodromes) present almost as much variety as road race courses, although there is a strong move to standardise the design of tracks used for major international competition. (The circumferences of the world's most famous bowls are now all between 250 and 333 m.)

Some, such as the temporary indoor tracks used for most six-day races, are extremely small (well under 200 m), with 'wall-of-death' bankings of 50° or more. Others are as big as 600 m and almost flat.

▲ *Defying gravity – centrifugal force keeps riders pinned to the steep banking*

The shape varies too. Many tracks from the Victorian and Edwardian eras survive to this day. Often they are D-shaped with a long finishing straight, sometimes wider than the rest of the track, to accommodate thrilling bunch finishes. The famed German architect, Schuurman, who built many tracks around the world in the fifties and sixties, favoured long straights and short steep bankings. Contemporary Australian designer, Ron Webb, prefers an almost oval shape, with short straights, long, flowing bankings, and a very smooth transition between the two. Such a design enables extremely fast racing to take place.

Surfaces also vary, calling for quite different tyres, tactics and techniques. Seasoned hardwood (usually from Africa) is the fastest, though asphalt and cement are most common. In the tropics, hard baked clay is sometimes used, and where no hard tracks exist, race meetings can be held on unbanked grass tracks.

Manchester's National Cycling Centre, ▶
designed by Ron Webb

Track riders can choose from an entire menu of events. Five or six quite distinctive kinds of race can be crammed into an afternoon or evening meeting of two or three hours. Rather than wait for their speciality, most competitors take part in a range of other events, though serious sprinters and pursuiters might ride just a single warm-up or warm-down distance race beside their favoured discipline.

Equipment

Track bikes are simple machines. Since there are no brakes or gears (just a single-speed fixed wheel) or feeding bottle cages, they can be considerably cheaper than road racing bikes.

However, we are now in an age of low-profile, superlight frames (made from aluminium, carbon fibre, titanium or other costly materials), expensive disc and tri-spokes, disc wheels and so on.

Many riders at track leagues around the country compete happily and reasonably successfully on second-hand bikes, though a new, basic, all-round track bike can cost only a few hundred dollars. However, top level competition in each discipline does demand rather different machinery, which will add to the basic cost.

A sprint bike needs a short wheelbase, a tight, very stiff rear triangle, plus rigid bars, stem and chainset to resist the enormous torque when the sprinter unleases his 'jump'. It also needs a high bottom-bracket to give plenty of ground clearance and reduce the risk of clipping a pedal on the banking: a common cause of low-speed crashes. Wheels need to be stiffly laced (preferably with spokes tied and soldered for extra strength).

While sprinters are preoccupied with responsiveness, the pursuiter, on the other hand, will seek to shed every possible ounce of superfluous weight from his machine.

A serious pursuiter might invest several thousand dollars in a low-profile, monocoque frame, and the lightest wheels and tyres. Some even test the whole ensemble in a wind tunnel.

Depending on the track, gears used for most events will range between 88 and 92 inches, increasing to 96, 98 or even higher for pursuiters. (Gears for juveniles are subject to restrictions, so check the USCF Annual Rule Book for appropriate rules. These books also include tables to help you calculate gear sizes correctly.)

◀ *The sprint bicycle (ridden by Michael Hubner, left) and the pursuiter's mount (Rob Hayles, right) have evolved into two very different machines* ▶

Spare wheels, sprockets and chain-rings, a good, heavy-duty track pump and a comprehensive tool-kit should all be part of your equipment. Given the poor facilities at so many tracks, a groundsheet to sit on and a supply of refreshments will help make life more pleasant. A good pair of rollers or a turbo trainer are also advisable for both warming up and warming down.

Clothing

Serious track riders opt now for one-piece skinsuits rather than separate track vest and shorts. With races being short, there's no need for food pockets.

Ensure that the shoe cleats are in good condition. Many 'trackies' prefer to ride without socks to prevent feet from slipping round inside shoes.

You can use the same crash helmet and shoes as for road racing, though special aerodynamic crash helmets are available for pursuiting. Leather 'hair net' crash helmets are no longer permitted. Now only hardshell helmets bearing the Snell or ANSI approval marks are acceptable.

Track mitts are vital for wiping grit from rolling tyres and to protect hands in case of crashes.

It also pays to wear something under the skinsuit. A silky track vest is ideal, but if not, a t-shirt will do. Should you be unlucky enough to fall, burns can often be avoided by the two garments sliding across each other and dissipating the friction.

Care should be taken when pinning on numbers to ensure they can be seen clearly by the judges and do not present gaping air pockets (carry extra safety pins).

Bring plenty of clothing such as sweat tops, track suit or leg warmers to wear between races. You can get very cold sitting around between events.

Sprinting

The Blue Riband cycle racing event, sprinting in its classic two-up format, is one of the purest forms of sport. Explosive power for fast acceleration to flat-out speed is crucial. But the champion sprinter must also ally this tremendous strength with suppleness and a quick mind. The very best are able to ride each race in a completely different fashion, never giving rivals a chance to latch on to a favourite tactic and thus plan how to counter it.

Recent rule changes, which have effectively outlawed the bumping, boring and leaning on which used to be an integral part of sprinting, have taken away some of the excitement, but a good sprint match is still a fascinating and thrilling crowd-pleaser.

At top level, sprints are run on a two-up (one rider against another) format over a distance of 1000 m, only the last 200 of which are timed. Local track league sprints, however, might put as many as six riders together for a one-lap dash.

Pure sprinting is a cat-and-mouse affair, with each rider trying to catch the other off-guard. The rider who draws inside position has to lead for the first lap at a minimum of walking pace. After that he will probably try to force his rival to go to the front by adopting the famous 'stand-still' tactic, using his fixed wheel drive to help balance the bike. Stand-stills can last mere seconds or run into minutes, although if either rider rolls back more than 10 cm the race will be restarted. The rear berth is favoured because it offers both shelter and the chance to launch a surprise attack. Some riders do, however, prefer to control things from the front.

Of course, you can go flat out right from the start. This tactic will pay off if you catch your opponent off-guard and open a really clear lead. If your rival manages to get onto your wheel, though, he will happily sit there, let you expend all your energy setting the pace, then easily overtake as you come up the home straight.

▲ *Marty Nothstein – America's sprinting great.*

In most sprints, the real action is compressed into the last three-quarters of a lap. One rider dives from high up the banking, while the other tries not only to follow, but also to get either the inside berth first or come over the top and squeeze down. Once inside the sprinters line (a mark which runs about a metre above the inside of the track), the lead rider must stay there and not wander out again unless he has at least a bike's length of clear lead. Favourite manoeuvres for the lead rider are to hold the rival pinned against the fence until the last possible minute or, should he go for the inside position, to come down hard and close the door.

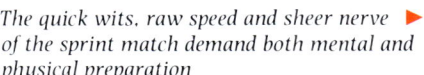

The quick wits, raw speed and sheer nerve of the sprint match demand both mental and physical preparation

◀ *A strong push and explosive start are essential in handicap racing. The author in action at Herne Hill in the 1970s*

Handicap racing

A derivative of sprinting, handicaps are very popular and have provided valuable schooling for generations of aspiring sprinters.

Competitors are given varying levels of start over the scratch mark. For open events, a national handicap–mark table is kept by the USCF, the scratch mark being the national sprint champion. If a visiting world champion competes, he is given a mark behind scratch. Riders with no previous recorded form, i.e. novices, are given a middlemarker's position for their debut. Throughout the season, starting marks are adjusted up or down according to a rider's performances.

The handicapper's dream is to have all the riders crossing the line together in a dead heat, and good handicapping does produce some wonderful racing. Longmarkers go flat-out from the start, trying to preserve enough of their advantage to win. Backmarkers start with an explosive effort, often with back tyres skipping as they strive to close the gap, weaving through the pack in a bid for the frontline and victory.

A good starting push is essential. Sneaky riders look for someone who will not only give them a hefty push, but who also has the knack of anticipating the starter's gun by a small enough margin for it not to be obvious. If noticed, a false-start is called. Good pushers are always in heavy demand at track meetings.

Start with your best foot not forward, but right at the top of the pedal cycle. The push will carry you over the hump, and then you will have a full 180° of downward pedal stroke available to provide a really fast start.

Block handicap

This is a longer distance handicap race, in which riders are started in small groups. It is especially popular in Australia, where events like The Golden Wheel offer very rich prizes.

Kilo

The kilometre is the event they all love to hate. A flying-start time trial over 1000 m, it is too long for a pure sprinter and too short for a pure pursuiter. It demands an all-out effort: start too slowly and you will never be in contention, yet do too much too early and you risk dying over the last lap. At the end, if you aren't gasping for breath, legs burning with effort, then you haven't tried hard enough.

▲ *The kilo demands flat out effort*

Tandem sprinting

For true track racing fans, this super high speed event, with its thrills and spectacular spills, is one of the best races of all. Sadly, however, it has recently been dropped from the world championship schedules due to a shortage of competitors (the high cost and rarity of track tandems being at the heart of the problem). A good pairing comprises a powerhouse stoker and a fearless steersman.

Thrills and spills of tandem sprinting from the 1971 World Championships ▶

Pursuiting

As a pure test of athletic prowess, top level pursuiting is one of the most glamorous forms of bike racing. With its close affinity to road time trialling, it is also one in which British riders have consistently been among the best in the world.

Technology reaches its zenith in this discipline. Low-profile frames, small front wheels, disc rear wheels and specially streamlined helmets are all expensive aids to achieving the most aerodynamic position possible. For years, this was a low tuck, dubbed 'the egg position'. Then triathlon exponents developed tri-bars, which clip on to normal handlebars. After starting on the drops, riders go onto their tri-bars, which enable them to tuck their arms in tight to their chest, presenting the least possible wind resistance. Scottish star Graeme Obree took this even further with his strange (now banned) hunched up position, which won him the world hour record and a world champion's rainbow jersey.

◀ *The classic pursuiting style of Gene Samuel*

Graeme Obree's now outlawed crouch ▶

▲ *Italy's perfectly drilled team pursuit squad at full bore*

Competitors start on opposite sides of the track, the objective being to beat the opponent, either by being faster over the full distance or by catching and eliminating him before the finish. Tactics are simply to pace oneself effectively.

Riders are held up at the start, but may not receive a push. At major events, this dead start is effected by a special starting gate, which requires a particular technique. If you are faced with one, ensure that you get some practice starts before the event.

Station pursuits are run with four or six riders on the track at the same time, placed at equidistant intervals. Riders who are caught are immediately eliminated from the event.

Team pursuit
Instead of matches between individuals, these pursuits involve teams of four. Each rider does a quarter, half or full lap at the front, dependent on the size of the track and the strength of the team's individual riders. After his turn, the lead rider swings high up the banking, allowing the next rider to hit the front. He then swings back down onto the tail of the team before the chain of riders revolves him to the front for his next turn. Smoothness is of the essence: do not accelerate as you go through, as this will make it difficult for the rider you are relieving to get back onto the string, and could well split the team apart.

Italian team pursuit
In this event between teams of five, each rider does a lap at the front then pulls out, eventually leaving just one rider from each team to fight out the final lap.

Olympic sprint
Not really a sprint at all, this event is an Italian pursuit but with just three riders in each team. It is one of the fastest and most thrilling of track events, and now has its own national and world championship titles.

Distance events

Scratch racing

Classic distances are five miles, 20 km (the national title distance) and 25 miles. These are straightforward, massed-start, bunched races, with the winner being the first to cross the line. The closest thing on the track to a road race, they call for similar riding style and tactics, except that there are no corners or hills, and you ride a single-speed, fixed wheel. The ability to pedal at high revs is important.

Bunch track races are a great place to learn bike-handling and following the wheels correctly. There are no brakes, so you have to correct speed by 'kicking back'.

An action-packed 10 mile scratch at the Commonwealth Games ▶

Points racing

A bunch race (championship distance is 40 km) in which the winner is the rider who amasses the greatest number of points in the sprints held at intervals throughout the event. Points are awarded 3-2-1 to the first three riders each lap, and are usually doubled on the final lap.

Riders who are far behind on points can still save the day: if they get away and lap the field then they automatically win.

Courses des primes

This race has no overall winner. Prizes are up for grabs in sprints, which are held either every lap or at set intervals through the event.

Devil take the hindmost

A race where the brain counts for as much or more than brawn, at least until the very final stage. Also known as the 'elimination' or 'miss and out', in this event the last rider (or sometimes the last two) at the end of each lap is pulled out, leaving a pre-determined number of riders (usually two or four) to fight out the final lap. Positioning is all-important, riders often being eliminated simply because they cannot find a gap to get through.

Leicester's famous boards rattle to a ▶ bunch race attack in the 1994 National Championships

There are two classic ways of riding such a race. You can either control it from the front (always keeping in the first two or three positions), or ride it from the back, picking on individual rivals and pinning them into a position, usually on the inside of the track, from which they cannot escape and come past. Devils call for great skill, especially the ability to squeeze safely through the tightest of gaps, and are tremendous crowd-pleasers.

Always remember that the judgement is made not on the front wheel but on the back wheel, so don't make the mistake of easing as your front wheel crosses the line.

A truly sadistic version of this event is the reverse devil, in which the winner of each lap drops out, leaving the weakest to ride the furthest!

Unknown distance
It could be one lap or it could go on for 30; nobody knows the distance they have to race over until one of the judges rings the bell for the last lap.

Hare and hounds
A distance race where the field is divided into two groups of roughly equal size, which start on opposite sides of the track. The bunch comprising the lesser riders are the hares, who get a half-lap start.

Track racing has always drawn huge crowds ▶

Madison

Named after New York's Madison Square Garden venue, a madison is points racing run relay fashion, and is disputed by two- (sometimes three-) man teams. Team-mates take turns in the race, usually riding two laps before changing with their partners, who meanwhile roll slowly round the outside of the track awaiting their turn. Changes are thrilling and potentially dangerous affairs. The rider being relieved switches his hold from the bottom of the bars to the centre of the tops. He then reaches out with his right hand to grab hands with his partner, who will have dropped down from the banking to pick up the right closing speed. The relieving rider is then hand-slung into the fray by his partner. In former times, changes were effected by grabbing a special pad sewn into the partner's shorts and then pushing him forward into the race.

Essentially interval training made competitive, even short madisons are gruelling affairs, with weaker teams often conceding many laps. Once lapped, however, they can again contest the points, which are decided at the head of the field.

Final positions of teams finishing in the same lap are decided by the number of points they have scored.

◀ *The classic handsling relay technique of Madison racing – Stan Tourne of Belgium throws his Russian partner, Krabzhov, into battle*

Six-day racing

In early days, six-day events found riders competing as individuals, without break, until the authorities banned such races as being 'inhuman'. It was then that the madison style of racing was devised. The rules were that one member of each team had to be on the track at all times, 24 hours a day. At night, though, the race was neutralised, with riders circling slowly while they steered with one foot, chatted, read the paper or even shaved!

To make the racing faster, more exciting and more civilised, the format has been gradually revised until now racing takes place in sessions, usually of around an hour's duration, with riders resting in between.

As well as the madison sessions or 'chases', there are additional special events such as motor-pace, points races and devils to keep the crowds happy. While the riders in 'the race to nowhere' take their rest breaks, guest riders take part in special, invitation events, which often include matches between the world's great sprinters.

A great carnival, the classic six is held mid-winter in a vast, smoke-filled, indoor auditorium packed with fans, for whom the beer, entertainments and socialising are almost as important as the racing.

Riders who make it onto the six-day circuit can expect high earnings and a high-profile public image. Disadvantages are having to perform despite physical exhaustion (while spectators are having a party!), and the demanding travel across Europe from one six-day venue to another.

◀ Six-day riders on their race to nowhere

Motor-pace

Once among the most popular sports in Europe, especially in Germany, France and Spain, motor-pacing is now in the doldrums and has even been dropped from the current world championship schedule.

Despite average speeds of up to 60 mph, such events, usually one-hour long, can turn into a boring procession. At its best, though, motor-pacing is a wonderful spectacle, calling for particular talents. While the rider must be able to ride smoothly and stick just inches away from the roller at the back of the pacing motorcycle, his pacer needs to be able to 'sense' the good and bad patches his charge will inevitably go through, and adjust speed and tactics to suit.

Overtaking, especially when three bikes are running abreast, is not just thrilling, it's when races can be won and lost. A good pacer knows how to place himself not only so his own rider gets maximum pacing advantage, but so that his slipstream will blow a rival rider off his roller. Fittingly, the world championship winning pacers, as well as their pace-followers, were always awarded both a champion's jersey and a medal.

To race behind the big motors you will need a special pacing bike with a very high gear, reversed front forks and a very small front wheel to optimise the pacing effect. Tyres are bound onto the rims with special tapes for safety (speeds can touch 70 mph at times).

However, smaller motorcycles and the famous Derny machines (effectively pedal cycles with a small engine) are used to pace races in which riders use conventional track bikes.

▼ *The highly specialised machine of motor-pace racing*

If you are truly foolhardy, with the thousands of dollars needed to mount a successful attempt, then you might one day fancy a crack at the world cycling landspeed record, in which unlimited pace is permitted. This involves riding behind a specially tuned, high–performance car fitted with a huge windshield at the back. The current record stands at close to 150 mph! Also there for the taking is the one–hour, standing–start, paced record of 122.862 km (76 miles 604 yds), established way back in 1928 by Belgian rider, Leon Vanderstuyft.

Now no longer on the calendar, the Bordeaux–Paris used to be the world's longest single-day road race. In its latter years, riders were paced by Dernys for most of the distance.

◀ *Once a major spectator draw, motor-pace is now declining in popularity*

Keirin

Japan's contribution to bike racing, apart from that wonderful Shimano equipment, is keirin racing. One of that country's most popular sports, it has an annual audience of more than 30 million and generates vast revenue from trackside gambling. In adapted form, keirin is now practised internationally and included in the world championships.

At the start of the race, usually six to eight riders are lined up on the inside of the track in their drawn order, which must be maintained for the first lap. After that they can jostle for their favoured position (usually number-two slot) behind the pacer. In Japan the pacer is another rider, elsewhere a motorcyclist, who gradually winds up the speed before peeling off with around three-quarters of a lap to go. Riders must not overtake him until he peels off, when they can fight out the finish amongst themselves.

Keirin calls for great bike-handling skills, an iron nerve and a touch of the bully-boy instinct, experts intimidating rivals to give way in the battle for best position.

▲ *Winding up the pace in a British keirin*

Riding in a bunch

The most important basic technique required for both road and track racing is the ability to ride safely and efficiently 'on the wheels'.

Practice, they say, makes perfect, and a good place to start is on club runs. It takes a bit of nerve, but you will soon get used to riding close up to the rider in front, just inches from his back wheel, and rubbing shoulders with the rider beside you.

It is safest to ride slightly to one side of the wheel you are following. In cross wind conditions, ride towards the leeward side to get maximum shelter. Avoid sharp braking, switching or 'kicking back' when getting out of the saddle, as these may endanger your fellow competitors.

Sharing the pace by working 'bit and bit' is also an acquired science. Avoid going through too fast, as this will only impair the efficiency of the group and cause gaps to open. Another common fault is to do too long a stint on the front, as this will tire you and tends to lower the pace. If you are feeling weak, just 'tap' through or sit at the back, but keep out of the way of those riders who are working.

▲ *Following the wheels correctly is essential in the big bunch of a major race like the Wincanton Classic*

Always swing off on the windward side, thus allowing the following riders to echelon (or fan out) effectively so that they are not out in the wind.

When sprinting, remember the quickest way to the line is the shortest way, and that while you are switching one rider out of contention, you might well be letting someone else nip through to rob you of victory.

Should you have a puncture or mechanical problems, raise your hand to warn other riders and any following spares vehicle.

Training

Training for cycle racing is a highly complex issue. To choose the right regime for you, bear in mind your own physical and psychological make-up, as well as precisely which discipline you wish to specialise in and, of course, how much time you can dedicate to it. Training is, however, a contentious issue, with every 'expert' having his own pet, and often highly debatable, theories.

Time was when 'miles, miles and more miles' was the training maxim. Today, though, we are more scientific in approach, using pulse meters, interval-type training, etc., in pursuit of quality rather than quantity. However, if you do intend to spend hours in the saddle on long races, then you must of course acclimatise your body to such distances.

Many cycling clubs have their own trainers. However, if yours does not, plenty of former and existing champions are happy to pass on their own advice in the numerous books on the subject. The more information you access, the more likely you are to come up with the right solution for you.

▲ *This most demanding sport pushes riders to their limits*

One thing is for certain though: you will not enjoy your bike racing unless you come to it with a high basic level of physical fitness. There is no getting away from the simple fact that you'll only get out what you put in, and hard work and sensible diet are essential. This, combined with a meticulously devised and followed training regime, will pay colossal dividends, as proven by the success of Chris Boardman.

Drugs

Drugs are the curse of modern sport, earning a high profile in cycling circles through a number of tragedies, including the death in the Tour de France of Britain's former world champion, Tom Simpson. Cycling was, however, the first sport to take the threat of drug abuse seriously and to impose a testing regime. Random tests are now held, not just in the racing environment, but at any time. Sophisticated detection methods are used and procedures continually refined to assure fairness.

The USCF issues a list of proscribed substances. Many of these occur in prescribed and patent medicines, so be sure to check that anything you are taking—even on doctor's orders—contains nothing listed as banned. Remember, ignorance is no excuse, and those found guilty of using banned substances face severe penalties.

Drug taking is not only cheating by seeking to gain an unnatural advantage, it is also dangerous and potentially life-threatening.

Glossary – bike talk

backmarker The scratch rider in a handicap event.
bidon A feeding bottle.
bit and bit A technique by which riders share the pace-making, each taking a short turn at the front of the group then swinging off to let the next rider through.
block The freewheel cluster.
breakaway or break An individual or group of riders with a clear lead.
chain gang An informally organised training group.
cleats The plates on the bottom of cycling shoes, which attach the shoe securely to the pedal.
criterium A road race held on a small circuit closed to all other traffic.
derailleur The gearing system of a road racing bike.
drops The lower curved section of racing handlebars.
echelon The fanning out of a group when riding in a crosswind.
fish and chipper A minor, relatively easy race, where the low prizes are scarcely worth enough to buy a fish supper!
grimpeur Climbing specialist.
group set An integrated set of cycle accessories, including gears, brakes and chainset.
jump A sprinter's explosive acceleration.
knock or bonk Nausea and total weakness due to sugar debt. Avoid it by feeding regularly during longer races or training rides.
longmarker The limit man, or rider with the biggest start in a handicap race.
musette A cotton bag used for handing food up to riders during long road races.
off the back When a rider is dropped by the bunch.
on the rivet Riding flat out. (Old-fashioned leather saddles had brass rivets on the nose. A rider making a big effort tends to slip to the front of the saddle.)
peloton The bunch or main group in a race.
prime A special mid-race lap or hill prize.
rouleur A strong time triallist or flat race specialist.
skinsuit One-piece racing garment comprising top and shorts, used by track riders and in time trials.
sling a hook When a sprinter nudges his rival off line.
soigneur A combination trainer, masseur, confidant.
sprints and tubs Specialised racing rims and tyres.
stayer A motor-pace race specialist.
through and off Another term for 'bit and bit'.
tri-bars Special handlebar grips which clip on to allow an extended crouch position for time trialling or pursuiting.
yellow jersey The name given to the race leader in a stage race (derived from the symbolic jersey awarded to the Tour de France race leader each day).

Useful addresses

U.S. Cycling Federation
1750 E. Boulder St. No. 4
Colorado Springs, CO 80909
phone: 719–578–4581

Bicycle Federation of America
1506 21st St. NW, Suite 200
Washington, D.C. 20036
phone: 202–463–6622
fax: 202–332–6989

American Bicycle Association
PO Box 718
Chandler, AZ 85244
phone: 602–961–1903

Index

address 46

backmarkers 29, 44
bidons 16, 44
bikes
   buying 11
   pacing 38
   pursuit 24, 31
   sprint 24
   track 24
bit and bit 41, 44
block handicap 29
Boardman, Chris 42
British Cycling
   Federation 8, 9

chain gangs 7, 44
cleats 11, 44
closed circuits 15
clothing 12, 25
club runs 41
clubs 7
competition categories 9
Coppi, Fausto 10, 11
courses des primes 34
cramp 13
criteriums 14, 44

devil take the hindmost
   34–5
distance events 33–5
drops 31, 44
drugs 43

echelon 41, 44
energy drinks 11
English Schools Cycling
   Association 8, 9
equipment 10, 24–5

fish and chippers 9, 44

gears 11, 24
glossary 44
group sets 11, 44

handicap racing 29
hare and hounds 35
helmets 12, 25

jerseys 12
jumps 24, 44
juvenile racing 16

keirin 40
kicking back 33, 41
kilo 29

licences 8
longmarkers 29, 44

madison 36
massage 13
motor-pace 38-9
musettes 16

Obree, Graeme 31

pedals 11
points racing 34
preparation 13
primes 15, 44
pursuits 31–2
   Italian team 32
   Olympic sprint 32
   team 32
race food 11
riding in a bunch 41
road racing 5, 8

saddles 12
scratch mark 29
scratch racing 33
shoes 12
shorts 12
single day racing 6, 16
skinsuits 25, 44
stage racing 7
stand-stills 26

tandem sprinting 30
time trials 8, 20–1
Tour de France 4, 5, 18
track mitts 12, 25
track racing 22
track vests 25
training 7, 42
tri-bars 31, 44
tyre pressure 11

unknown distance 35

velodromes 22–3

yellow jersey 6, 7, 44